Rethinking International Drug Control: New Directions for U.S. Policy

Report
of an Independent Task Force

Sponsored by the Council on Foreign Relations
Mathea Falco, Chair

The Council on Foreign Relations, Inc., is a nonprofit and nonpartisan organization devoted to promoting improved understanding of international affairs through the free exchange of ideas.

The Council on Foreign Relations takes no institutional position on policy issues and has no affiliation with the U.S. government. This report is the sole responsibility of the Task Force.

From time to time, the Council will select a topic of critical importance to U.S. policy to be the subject of study by an independent, nonpartisan Task Force. The Council chooses members representing diverse views and backgrounds, including generalists as well as experts. Many, but not all, Task Force members are also members of the Council.

This study benefited from the advice of Task Force members as well as from the discussions of Council groups convened for one session each in Los Angeles, Chicago, Miami, and Atlanta. The statement reflects the policy judgments of the Task Force members, although not every member necessarily subscribes to every aspect.

For further information about the Council or this Task Force, please contact the Public Affairs Office, Council on Foreign Relations, 58 East 68th Street, New York, NY 10021.

For additional background material on international drug control policy, please contact Drug Strategies, 2445 M Street, NW, Suite 480, Washington, DC 20037; phone 202-663-6090, fax 202-663-6110. Drug Strategies is a nonprofit, policy research institute supported by several national foundations.

CONTENTS

MEMBERS OF THE TASK FORCE

BRUCE M. BAGLEY: Dr. Bagley is Professor of International Relations at the Graduate School of International Studies, University of Miami.

DAVID BEALL*: Mr. Beall is Executive Secretary of the Inter-American Drug Abuse Control Commission (CICAD) at the Organization of American States (OAS).

EVERETT BRIGGS: Ambassador Briggs is President of the Americas Society and the Council of the Americas. He served as U.S. Ambassador to Panama, Honduras and Portugal; Deputy Assistant Secretary of State for Inter-American Affairs; and Special Assistant to the President for Latin America and the Caribbean at the National Security Council.

JAMES E. BURKE: Mr. Burke is Chairman of the Partnership for a Drug-Free America and former Chairman of Johnson & Johnson.

ROBERT CARSWELL: Mr. Carswell is Partner at Shearman & Sterling and Chairman of the Carnegie Endowment for International Peace. He served as Deputy Secretary of the Treasury from 1977-1981.

---

* Individual participated in the Task Force discussions but was not asked to endorse the statement or the background study because of his or her official capacity.

Note: Institutional affiliations listed for identification purposes only.

JONATHAN A. CHANIS: Mr. Chanis is Managing Director of AIG Capital Partners, Inc.

W. BOWMAN CUTTER: Mr. Cutter is Managing Director at E. M. Warburg, Pincus, and Co. in New York. He has served as Deputy Assistant to the President for Economic Policy, the National Economic Council at the White House.

MARK DANNER: Mr. Danner is staff writer at *The New Yorker* magazine and author of *The Massacre at El Mozote* (Vintage, 1994). He is writing a book on Haiti and is author of two ABC-TV News documentaries: "While America Watched: The Bosnia Tragedy" and "House on Fire: America's Haitian Crisis."

MATHEA FALCO: Ms. Falco is President of Drug Strategies, a nonprofit institute to promote effective approaches to substance abuse. The author of *The Making of A Drug- Free America: Programs that Work* (Times Books, 1994), she was Assistant Secretary of State for International Narcotics Matters from 1977 to 1981.

STEPHEN E. FLYNN*: Dr. Flynn is a Lieutenant Commander in the U.S. Coast Guard and Military Professor of International Relations at the Coast Guard Academy. In 1991, he was selected as the Coast Guard's first Council on Foreign Relations' International Affairs Fellow.

SERGIO GALVIS: Mr. Galvis is Partner at Sullivan & Cromwell, where he coordinates the firm's Latin American practice.

EDUARDO A. GAMARRA: Dr. Gamarra is Director of Graduate Programs at the Latin American and Caribbean Center at Florida International University, where he is also Associate Professor of Political Science and editor of *Hemisphere Magazine*.

SUSAN GINSBURG*: Ms. Ginsburg is Senior Advisor for Enforcement at the Department of the Treasury.

PETER HAKIM: Mr. Hakim is President of the Inter-American Dialogue.

MARGARET A. HAMBURG, M.D.*: Dr. Hamburg is Commissioner of Health for New York City and serves as Vice-Chairperson of the Board of Drug Strategies.

ALBERTO HART*: Mr. Hart is Deputy Secretary of the Inter-American Drug Abuse Control Commission (CICAD) at the Organization of American States (OAS).

---

* Individual participated in the Task Force discussions but was not asked to endorse the statement or the background study because of his or her official capacity.

Note: Institutional affiliations listed for identification purposes only.

CLIFFORD KRAUSS*: Mr. Krauss is outgoing Chief of the *New York Times* Police Department Bureau. He has also reported on the State Department and Congress and is author of *Inside Central America: Its People, Politics and History* (Summit, 1991).

JEFFREY LAURENTI: Mr. Laurenti is Executive Director of Policy Studies at the United Nations Association of the United States of America, and author of *Breaking the Drug Chain: Options for International Policy on Narcotic Drugs* (UNA-USA, 1990).

RENSSELAER LEE: Dr. Lee is President of Global Advisory Services, a research company specializing in international development and security issues. He is the author of *The White Labyrinth: Cocaine and Political Power* (Transaction, 1989) and co-author of *The Andean Cocaine Industry* (St. Martins Press, 1996).

ELIZABETH LEEDS: Dr. Leeds is Executive Director of the Center for International Studies at the Massachusetts Institute for Technology.

KENNETH MAXWELL: Dr. Maxwell is Nelson and David Rockefeller Senior Fellow for Inter-American Affairs and Director of the Latin America Program at the Council on Foreign Relations.

ROBERT B. MILLMAN, M.D.: Dr. Millman is Saul P. Steinberg Distinguished Professor of Psychiatry and Public Health at Cornell University Medical College and Director of Drug and Alcohol Abuse Programs at New York Hospital-Payne Whitney Psychiatric Clinic.

ANNE NELSON: Ms. Nelson is International Coordinator, Columbia Graduate School of Journalism, and former Executive Director of the Committee to Protect Journalists.

HERBERT S. OKUN*: Ambassador Okun is the U.S. member and First Vice-President of the United Nations International Narcotics Control Board (INCB). He has served as U.S. Ambassador to East Germany and to the United Nations.

HOLLY PETERSON: Ms. Peterson is Domestic Policy Producer for ABC-TV's World News Tonight.

RENATE RENNIE: Ms. Rennie is President of The Tinker Foundation Incorporated.

PETER REUTER: Dr. Reuter is Professor in the School of Public Affairs and Department of Criminology at the University of Maryland. From 1989 to 1993 he was Co-Director of RAND's Drug Policy Research Center.

---

* Individual participated in the Task Force discussions but was not asked to endorse the statement or the background study because of his or her official capacity.

Note: Institutional affiliations listed for identification purposes only.

K. JACK RILEY*: Dr. Riley is Acting Director of the Drug Use Forecasting/Arrestee Drug Abuse Monitoring program at the U.S. Department of Justice, National Institute of Justice. He is author of *Snow Job? The War Against International Cocaine Trafficking* (Transaction, 1996).

ROBERTO SALINAS-LEÓN: Dr. Salinas-León is Executive Director of the Centro de Investegaciones Sobre la Libre Empresa (Center for Free Market Research), Mexico city. He is also Adjunct Professor of Political Economy in the Escuela Libra de Derecho and a member of the Mont Pelerin Society.

PETER H. SMITH: Dr. Smith is Professor of Political Science, Simon Bolivar Professor of Latin American Studies, and Director of Latin American Studies at the University of California, San Diego.

HERBERT STURZ: Mr. Sturz is President of The Trotwood Corporation and is on the Board of Drug Strategies. He was founding Director of the Vera Institute of Justice, and also served as New York City Deputy Mayor of Criminal Justice and as Chairman of the New York City Planning Commission.

WILLIAM J. VANDEN HEUVEL: Ambassador van-den Heuvel is former U.S. Deputy Permanent Representative to the United Nations and was Special Assistant to Attorney General Robert F. Kennedy. He is Counsel to the law firm of Stroock & Stroock & Lavan and Senior Advisor to Allen & Company Incorporated.

JONATHAN M. WINER*: Mr. Winer is Deputy Assistant Secretary of State for International Narcotics and Law Enforcement Affairs.

Rapporteur
JOHN M. WALSH-ALKER: Mr. Walsh-Alker is a consultant to Drug Strategies and a graduate student at The Johns Hopkins University Institute for Policy Studies in Baltimore. He was Special Assistant for U.S. International Drug Policy at the Washington Office on Latin America (WOLA) from 1990 to 1993.

---

* Individual participated in the Task Force discussions but was not asked to endorse the statement or the background study because of his or her official capacity.

Note: Institutional affiliations listed for identification purposes only.

PRESENTERS AT
TASK FORCE MEETINGS

BRUCE M. BAGLEY*: Dr. Bagley is Professor of International Relations at the Graduate School of International Studies, University of Miami.

JAMIE FELLNER: Ms. Fellner is Associate Counsel of Human Rights Watch and directs its project addressing the human rights implications of national and international drug policies. She is author of two recent Human Rights Watch reports on drug policy and human rights in Bolivia.

ROBERT S. GELBARD: Ambassador Gelbard is Assistant Secretary of State for International Narcotics and Law Enforcement Affairs. A career Foreign Service Officer, he was also Ambassador to Bolivia and Principal Deputy Assistant Secretary of State for Inter-American Affairs.

ERNEST T. PATRIKIS: Mr. Patrikis is First Vice President of the Federal Reserve Bank of New York. He is an alternate member of the Federal Open Market Committee and is responsible for the Wholesale Payments Product Office.

MIGUEL RUIZ-CABAÑAS: Mr. Ruiz-Cabañas is Coordinator for Special Affairs and Drug Control at the Mexican Foreign Ministry. A career diplomat, he has served as Mexico's Director General for United Nations Affairs and as Chief of Staff of the Deputy Foreign Minister.

---

* Task Force Members

PETER H. SMITH*: Dr. Smith is Professor of Political Science, Simon Bolivar Professor of Latin American Studies, and Director of Latin American Studies at the University of California, San Diego.

PAUL STARES: Dr. Stares is Senior Fellow in Foreign Policy Studies at the Brookings Institution and author of *Global Habit: The Drug Problem in a Borderless World* (Brookings, 1996).

FRANCISCO THOUMI: Dr. Thoumi is a Fellow at the Smithsonian's Woodrow Wilson Center for Scholars, where he is writing a book on the political economy of illegal drugs in the Andes. He is author of *Political Economy and Illegal Drugs in Colombia* (Lynne Rienner, 1995).

PHIL WILLIAMS: Dr. Williams is Director of the University of Pittsburgh's Ridgway Center for International Security Studies and Professor at the Graduate School of Public and International Affairs. He is editor of the journal *Transnational Organized Crime* and serves as a consultant to the United Nations Drug Control Program.

COLETTA YOUNGERS: Ms. Youngers is a Senior Associate with the Washington Office on Latin America (WOLA), where she analyzes human rights, political developments, and the impact of U.S. policy in the Andean region, especially Bolivia, Colombia and Peru.

FOREWORD

In the post-Cold War world, where America's international interests are often viewed through the filter of domestic concerns, drug control plays an increasingly important role in Washington's foreign policy formulation. This issue affects bilateral relations with more than a dozen countries, particularly in Latin America, the primary source for cocaine and much of the heroin coming into the United States. To examine the intersection of domestic and international interests, the Council on Foreign Relations convened an Independent Task Force of experts from many disciplines to review U.S. international drug strategy and to suggest possible future directions.[1] During the course of the year, the Task Force assessed the results of U.S. interdiction and source country efforts on America's drug problems as well as their impact in foreign countries. A central question for the Task Force was the extent to which these efforts advance U.S. foreign policy interests and/or achieve domestic policy goals.

Task Force members included both Council members and non-members drawn from diverse disciplines, with backgrounds in banking, law enforcement, diplomacy, journalism, economic development, public health, judicial institutions, human rights, and multinational business. Prominent academics, government officials, and policy experts presented a wide range of perspectives for the group's consideration. Drug Strategies, a nonprofit research institute in Washington, D.C., pro-

---

[1] The Task Force did not discuss legalization as an alternative strategy.

1

vided staff support for the project, which was funded by a grant from the John D. and Catherine T. MacArthur Foundation. The statement reflects the views of those who participated in the Task Force, except as indicated in additional and dissenting views. The background study was circulated to all participants and benefited from their advice and suggestions.

The Task Force met four times at the Council in New York. The Council also convened meetings in Los Angeles, Chicago, Miami, and Atlanta to discuss U.S. international drug control policy. More than one hundred people participated in Task Force discussions, reflecting the depth of interest in these issues. Brief summaries of the regional perspectives provided by the meetings and names of participants appear at the end of this report. This project was greatly assisted by the staffs of the Latin American Program and the National Program of the Council on Foreign Relations, to whom the Task Force extends special thanks.

Mathea Falco
Chair

February 1997

2

STATEMENT OF THE TASK FORCE

In the past two decades, much has been learned about international drug control. Based on its review of U.S. efforts to curtail foreign drug production and trafficking, the Task Force believes that a major shift in strategic thinking is needed so that U.S. policy can more effectively address the nation's drug problems.

Reassess the Effectiveness of Interdiction
Since 1981, Americans have spent more than $25 billion for foreign interdiction and source country programs intended to reduce the supplies of drugs coming into this country. These programs have created problems of their own, including strained relations with other countries, particularly in Latin America; political unrest and violence among peasant farmers who rely on drug crops for their livelihood; human rights abuses as governments try to suppress drug cultivation; increased corruption among local police forces; and expanding roles for the military in internal security and drug enforcement in countries where democracy is still fragile.

More important, from a U.S. perspective, these programs do not seem to have succeeded in reducing drug supplies in this country. Despite impressive seizures at the border, on the high seas, and in other countries, foreign drugs are cheaper and more readily available in the United States today than two decades ago. While current U.S. efforts send an important message that the United States will not allow drug traffickers to operate with impunity, we should not hold unreasonable expectations that interdiction will keep significant amounts of drugs out of this country or that overseas supply reduction programs will solve America's drug problems. The record is clear: for twenty years, these programs have done little more than rearrange the map of drug production and trafficking. Moreover, domestic production of illegal drugs is increasing, suggesting that American sources could potentially meet future foreign shortfalls, if any occur. Nonetheless, U.S. spending on interdiction and source country programs in Fiscal Year 1997 represents a 30 percent increase over 1996 levels and the President's proposed Fiscal Year 1998 budget includes substantial new funds for source country programs, primarily for Peru.

Strengthen Democratic Institutions
The United States has vital interests in attacking the power and profits of the multinational drug cartels that challenge the integrity of political, financial and judicial institutions in this country and abroad. Powerful narcocriminal networks undermine the future of democratic governments, particularly in this hemisphere. The Task Force believes that U.S. drug control policy should balance efforts to reduce foreign drug production and trafficking with greater emphasis on efforts to strengthen democratic institutions in countries threatened by these narcocriminal networks.

Target Money Laundering
Further, the Task Force believes that the United States should increase efforts to combat money laundering and drug-related corruption. The worldwide drug traffic generates as much as $400 billion annually: money

laundering, which allows traffickers to hide their profits, has itself become big business. Although the Administration has taken important first steps attacking these illegal financial flows, the Federal budget spends more for source country programs—aimed at the lowest level of the drug trafficking ladder—than for international programs to target high-end money laundering. Multilateral initiatives are particularly useful in this context, encouraging a global response to the global political, financial and economic aspects of drug trafficking.

Rethink Certification
The annual certification process, whereby the United States determines whether other countries have cooperated fully with U.S. drug control efforts, appears to have a number of problems. The criteria are vague and inconsistently applied, while the punishments are often more apparent than real. More important, the process itself is corrosive in its effects on U.S. relations with other countries, which often have a complex of problems that cannot be effectively addressed by this type of intervention. The Task Force suggests that Congress explore ways to ensure that nations are periodically assessed as to their performance in controlling illegal drug production, traffic, and money laundering without linking this to automatic penalties and without having the United States as the sole judge. Since illicit drugs are now a global problem, broadly based international bodies should be willing and able to undertake the task, perhaps with assistance from U.S. agencies that have special competence. If the Congress wishes to impose sanctions on a particular

nation as a result of this assessment, then it can do so. Moreover, this change would remove a recurring source of tension in U.S. relationships with Latin American countries where the annual certification debate often exacerbates nationalistic anti-American sentiment.

Develop Multilateral Efforts

While U.S. strategies have continued to emphasize unilateral or bilateral efforts internationally, drugs have become a global problem requiring global solutions. We cannot, and should not, do the job alone. International interdiction efforts could increasingly be multilateralized through greater emphasis on the concept of shared responsibility among all countries concerned. The need for multilateralizing the international effort is especially strong in areas where the United States and others must devote greater efforts, such as combating money laundering, control of precursor chemicals, and building better judicial and law enforcement institutions. Stronger legal systems are needed to protect democratic institutions in countries threatened by growing drug-related corruption. A multilateral approach is especially important in Latin America, where any perception that the United States is imposing solutions can be a negative political force working against international drug control objectives.

Reduce Domestic Demand

The Task Force believes that reducing the domestic demand for drugs is key in achieving sustained progress against drug abuse in this country. As the experience of the past two decades demonstrates, demand serves as a magnet to drug dealers everywhere who will find ways to supply America's lucrative market—despite our best efforts to curtail foreign drug production and trafficking. Education and prevention are particularly important: national surveys confirm a direct correlation between public perception of the risks of drug use and significantly lowered rates of use. Community law enforcement is also important, both in making neighborhoods safer and in driving up retail drug prices. Sustained, intensive, rigorous treatment has proved effective in curbing both drug addiction and drug crime. As Office of National Drug Control Policy (ONDCP) Director General Barry McCaffrey concluded in a January 1997 National Public Radio interview, "If there is a single issue that I need to support, it is to better argue for treatment capabilities that can address this chronic relapsing disorder and to persuade men

Federal Drug Control Budget

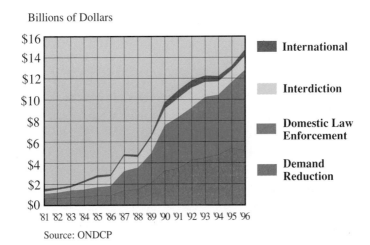

Billions of Dollars

International

Interdiction

Domestic Law Enforcement

Demand Reduction

'81 '82 '83 '84 '85 '86 '87 '88 '89 '90 '91 '92 '93 '94 '95 '96

Source: ONDCP

and women in public life, in Congress, state legislatures and city councils that effective drug treatment programs can markedly diminish the malignancy of drug abuse on cities and communities." Demand reduction programs currently receive about one-third of total Federal drug control funding. The Task Force believes that we need a more efficient approach to the nation's drug problems—one which will achieve greater results at less cost. This will involve rethinking our international drug control priorities.

BACKGROUND STUDY

International drug control policy intersects both foreign and domestic interests. U.S. drug control initiatives abroad are intended to produce direct domestic benefits, primarily reductions in drug availability, drug abuse and drug-related crime. Most U.S. foreign policy makers do not involve themselves with domestic drug abuse concerns, while prevention, treatment and law enforcement experts are often reluctant to engage in discussions of the foreign policy dimensions of drug control. Each group defers to the expertise of the other. As a result, analyses of international and domestic drug control priorities are rarely well integrated.

The Task Force review is timely in view of the growing importance of drug control relative to other U.S. foreign policy objectives, particularly in Latin America. Controlling illicit drugs has become a significant issue in U.S. dealings with a number of countries where Cold War concerns about Communist expansionism once dominated the bilateral agenda. A case in point is Pakistan, which emerged as a major illegal opium and heroin producer during the lengthy Soviet war in Afghanistan in the 1980s. Pakistan's role as a key ally assisting U.S.-financed cross-border operations into neighboring Afghanistan took priority over drug control issues in U.S. relations with Islamabad. With the Soviet threat ended, however, drug control is now close to the top of Washington's bilateral agenda with Pakistan.

In Latin America during the 1970s and 1980s, countering perceived Soviet and Cuban initiatives often overrode other U.S. foreign policy goals. With the demise of the former Soviet Union, Cuba's preoccupation with domestic problems, and the disappearance of military dictatorships in the region, Latin American drug control has received increasing attention from U.S. policy makers. That shift in emphasis was signaled in December 1989, when President George Bush ordered the military invasion of Panama, which the Administration justified in part by General Manuel Noriega's alleged involvement in drug trafficking.

Since the end of the Cold War, Washington's drug control assistance to Latin America has increased while economic development and military assistance has declined. United States annual foreign assistance to Latin America and the Caribbean fell from $1.7 billion in 1986 to $650 million in 1996. In contrast, narcotics related assistance to that region more than doubled during the same period, rising from $60 million to $134 million per year. U.S. anti-drug assistance now comprises 20 percent of total bilateral U.S. aid to Latin America, compared with only 3 percent a decade ago.

According to a 1995 Chicago Council on Foreign Relations survey, 85 percent of the U.S. public believes that stopping the flow of illegal drugs into the United States should be our most important foreign policy goal, ahead of protecting the jobs of American workers, preventing the spread of nuclear weapons, and controlling illegal immigration. Assistant Secretary of State Robert Gelbard captured this view in recent Congressional hearings when he testified that "in the post-Cold War world, you can hardly find a foreign policy issue that has such an immediate and direct detrimental effect on so many Americans as the international drug trade."

During the 1996 Presidential election campaign both Senator Dole and President Clinton pledged to do more to seal America's borders against illegal drugs and to cut off foreign drug production in response to government reports of escalating teen drug use. If teen drug use continues to rise, domestic political pressure for international solutions will probably increase. In seeking those solutions, U.S. international drug policy should reflect more accurately the growing complexities of global drug trends as well as the importance of reducing demand for drugs within this country.

U.S. efforts to cut off supplies of foreign drugs through interdiction and crop substitution in source countries have not reduced the availability of drugs in this country. Despite impressive, well-publicized tactical successes, these supply reduction initiatives have been overwhelmed by expanded drug production and increasingly sophisticated trafficking methods fueled by continuing worldwide demand for drugs.

The Task Force believes that the strategies of past decades, built on a world view divided into producer and consumer nations, are largely ineffective in achieving their purpose of reducing drug supplies coming into the United States. New realities call for a fundamental shift in thinking about U.S. foreign policy interests related to drug control and how to realize them through bilateral and multilateral initiatives that strengthen legitimate institutions in countries threatened by illicit drug production and trafficking. The

11

Task Force hopes that its work will contribute to shaping a more effective framework for future U.S. and multilateral international drug control efforts.

ILLEGAL DRUGS:
A COMPLEX GLOBAL PROBLEM

Drug trafficking is one of the world's most lucrative commercial activities. Current estimates of the value of all retail sales of illicit drugs range from $100 to $400 billion annually. Growth of the international drug market from cottage industry to a multi-billion dollar global trade can be traced to the massive surge in demand for drugs in the United States and Western Europe during the 1960s and 1970s. That surge triggered a rapid expansion in worldwide drug production and trafficking to meet the demands of those growing markets. Meanwhile, improvements in communications, transportation and information technology have made international borders more porous. Illicit drugs, like licit goods, services, money and people, now move across international boundaries with unprecedented speed and efficiency.

Globalization has also profoundly affected the incentives and opportunities to produce, traffic and consume drugs. Diffusion of technical expertise has made it possible to cultivate and refine drugs in distant places, while the expansion in trade, transportation and tourism has made it easier to distribute drugs to far-flung markets. Moreover, the growing integration of the global financial system has provided drug traffickers with many more opportunities to launder illicit profits. The immensity of those profits gives major drug trafficking organizations the power to subvert economies, democratic institutions and, in some cases, entire governments.

For much of this century, the illegal drugs used by Americans were produced abroad in a small number of countries. The United States targeted these source countries with diplomatic pressure as well as economic and enforcement assistance in return for their cooperation. For example, in 1969 President Richard Nixon closed a key crossing on the U.S.-Mexican border to force Mexico to take action against heroin and marijuana production, which were then supplying America's burgeoning illicit drug market. Subsequently, the United States provided more than $100 million to support the Mexican government's herbicide-spraying crop eradication campaign, an effort which reduced Mexico's opium and marijuana production during the late 1970s. President Nixon also threatened to cut off foreign assistance to Turkey unless that country stopped producing opium which supplied the 'French Connection' traffickers, then the primary source of heroin entering the United States. The Turkish government banned traditional opium cultivation but subsequently allowed a limited number of farmers to cultivate the more easily controlled *papaver bracteatum*, which requires a major industrial process to extract its narcotic. With $50 million in U.S. assistance, Ankara helped find alternative livelihoods for farmers disadvantaged by its new policies.

Successes in Turkey and Mexico were short-lived, however, as traffickers in Asia and the Middle East quickly increased production and developed alternative smuggling routes to supply the American and Western European heroin market. That pattern has continued, only now on a larger scale. Effective enforcement at one point in the supply chain brings about the opening of new fronts. As the U.S. Coast Guard's Pacific commander, Vice Admiral Roger T. Rufe, Jr., observed about drug interdiction in the January 30, 1997 *Washington Post*, "When you press the balloon in one area, it pops up in another....It's a market economy; with demand as it is in the U.S., they have plenty of incentive to try other routes."

Distinctions Between Drug Producing and Consuming Nations Are Fading
The United States, which is the world's largest drug market in terms of revenue, has traditionally been defined as a consumer country. According to the National Household Survey on Drug Abuse, 22.7 million Americans reported using illegal drugs at least once in 1995, while 12.8 million used drugs regularly (once a month or more).[2]

America's drug habit has historically been supplied from foreign sources: cocaine and marijuana from Latin America and the Caribbean; heroin from Southeast Asia's Golden Triangle (Burma, Laos, and Thailand) and South Asia's Golden Crescent (Afghanistan, Pakistan, and Iran). However, in recent years, a substantial percentage of American demand has been met by illegal domestic production. In particular, the drugs gaining popularity among teenagers—

---

[2] Three-quarters of these regular abusers are employed and three-quarters are white.

marijuana, methamphetamine, and LSD—are produced here at home as well as imported.

Drug Use Rising Among 8th Graders

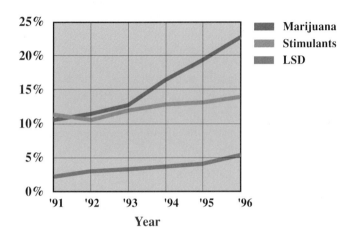

Source: Monitoring the Future Study

While most of our marijuana continues to be imported through Mexico and the Caribbean, domestic production now supplies an estimated one-quarter to one-half of America's consumption. Although a complete nationwide survey of illegal marijuana cultivation has not been made, U.S. officials report major cultivation areas in states as diverse as New York, Kentucky, California and Hawaii. Increased indoor cultivation, which allows for more selective hybridization, has accelerated the trend toward higher-potency marijuana. In 1996, the THC (tetrahydrocannabinol) content of high-grade "sinsemilla" (seedless) marijuana ranged from 12 to 24 percent, according to the Drug

Enforcement Administration (DEA), compared to less than 2 percent THC in marijuana cultivated in the early 1970s. Even as potency has increased, marijuana prices, after rising during the 1980s, have in the 1990s fallen back to levels of the early 1980s. Depending upon quality, marijuana now sells for roughly the same as its price in 1982—as little as $40 per ounce, although prices for high quality 'boutique' marijuana strains can reach $900 per ounce.

Meanwhile, traditional drug producing countries have also become drug consumers. Indigenous use of local drug crops (opium and coca) has been prevalent in certain regions for generations. For example, the hill tribes of Burma, Laos and Thailand have traditionally smoked and eaten opium to ease pain, hunger, and dysentery. So, too, have indigenous farmers and miners in Bolivia and Peru chewed coca leaves to ward off fatigue, altitude sickness, and hunger. Cultural practices as well as expense generally precluded local use of heroin and cocaine refined from opium and coca crops.

Over the past decade, however, secondary markets for heroin and cocaine in traditional societies have spread rapidly, made possible by expanded worldwide drug production and falling prices. Asian opium producing countries have increasing numbers of heroin addicts. China, where the Communist leadership used draconian measures to eliminate widespread addiction in the early 1950s, once again faces a growing drug problem. Supplied by opium produced and refined in northern Burma and China's southern Yunnan province, the People's Republic of China now has nearly 400,000 heroin addicts, according to Chinese officials. Western observers believe the actual number may be as high as four million.

In South America's Andean countries, the smoking of coca paste (known as *basuco*) is increasing, especially among children and teenagers. Cocaine use, once portrayed by Latin American governments as an exclusively North American vice, is also spreading. In Bolivia, by some estimates, 300,000 people used cocaine in 1994 compared to 25,000 in 1979—a twelvefold increase in 15 years. Ready drug availability, lower prices, and broad societal pressures have combined to convert many producer countries into consumers of their own products.

Traditional categories have also blurred with regard to transit countries. A particularly striking example is Mexico, which in the late 1960s and 1970s was a primary producer of the heroin and marijuana coming into this country. During that period, the United States concentrated much of its drug control funding on cooperative drug eradication programs in Mexico, which for a few years succeeded in reducing overall Mexican drug production. It did not, however, put Mexican traffickers out of business. In the mid-1980s, the United States Caribbean interdiction strategy, designed to prevent cocaine and marijuana from coming into South Florida, essentially pushed the Colombian cocaine cartels into finding new routes through Mexico. As one Latin American scholar noted at a Task Force meeting, "the influx of Colombian cocaine money transformed small-time Mexican drug families into world-class drug cartels." In addition to becoming a key transit route for South American drugs, Mexico has remained a major producer of heroin and marijuana for the U.S.

market and has become a source for the primary precursor to methamphetamine.

Drug Cultivation Is Rapidly Expanding Worldwide
Drug crops can be cultivated easily and cheaply almost anywhere in the world, as can be seen from the increased number of countries producing drugs over the past two decades.[3] Although coca has long been a traditional crop in Peru and Bolivia, which together account for three-quarters of world production, it is now grown in other South American countries with no

Drug Cultivation In Colombia

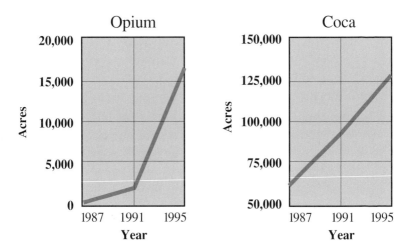

Source: Department of State INCSR 1996

---

[3] Production measures for illicit drugs are, of course, only rough estimates. The geographical remoteness that favors illicit crop cultivation also hinders researchers from accurately measuring the level of illegal production. Growers and marketers have obvious incentives to conceal their activities, and governments themselves may exaggerate or underestimate drug production and trafficking in their countries in order either to attract foreign aid or to avoid sanctions.

previous history of coca cultivation. Opium poppy, too, has spread to non-traditional areas. Before 1991, opium cultivation in Colombia had been negligible, but when cocaine profit margins fell during the late 1980s, Colombian traffickers diversified into producing heroin from locally grown poppies. Opium cultivation spread rapidly. According to DEA estimates, by 1996 Colombia was supplying 60 percent of the heroin coming into the United States. At the same time, farmers in Peru and Venezuela also started growing opium commercially in addition to coca.

Drug crops are the mainstay of some poor countries, where farmers have few economic alternatives. In Bolivia, with an annual per capita gross domestic product (GDP) of about $770, an acre of coca yields its grower about $475 yearly. That has proved a far more attractive return than prices ranging from $35-$250 an acre for crops such as bananas or grapefruit, which are far more susceptible to spoilage than coca. In 1992, coca generated an estimated $450 million in export revenues, equivalent to about 9 percent of Bolivia's GDP.

In the newly independent Central Asian states, most of which have high unemployment, weak economies and low standards of living, opium has become an important revenue source. One hectare (2.47 acres) of poppies can produce 20 times the income of a hectare of cotton, Central Asia's most important cash crop, and 35 times the income of a hectare of vegetables. In Kyrgyzstan, for example, where per capita gross national product (GNP) was only $610 in 1994, a pound of opium brings $400 in local markets or can be bartered for canned goods, cooking oil and other commodities. Opium production in Tajikistan, Turkmenistan and Uzbekistan has doubled since 1990.

Drug Trafficking Undermines Political, Financial and Economic Institutions
Profits from drug trafficking have grown enormously over the past two decades. The drug industry, no longer limited to local or regional "families" or "cartels," is serviced by sophisticated legal and financial professionals, a few of whom manage cash flows larger than the annual budgets of many small nations. Drug traffickers buy political influence, corrupt governments and distort economies, threatening democratic institutions—especially in developing countries.

Drug traffickers and other transnational criminal syndicates are undermining the political and economic development of newly independent countries in Central Asia, Eastern Europe and Russia. Burgeoning entrepreneurs in those countries have learned that hard drugs are a ready substitute for hard currency on the world market. Of particular concern are inroads by criminal enterprises into the Russian banking system, which allows them access to facilities for laundering illicit profits of all kinds, including from drugs.

In Southeast Asia, the Burmese economy is thought to rely heavily on the drug trade, according to a June 1996 report by the U.S. Embassy in Rangoon. Some politicians and generals in neighboring Thailand and Laos are believed to have links to the drug trade. In 1992, for example, intense U.S. pressure blocked influential Thai politician Narong Wongwan, alleged to be involved in drug trafficking, from becoming Prime Minister of Thailand.

In this hemisphere, the power of drug traffickers undermines fragile democratic institutions. In Colombia, the world's primary cocaine producer, illicit drugs help finance guerrilla insurgency in the countryside as well as subvert many governmental institutions in the cities. Reports of drug corruption among politicians in Colombia have long been common. Allegations that President Ernesto Samper accepted cartel money in the 1994 election campaign contributed to U.S. "decertification" of Colombia in 1996.[4] Colombia's judiciary has been seriously compromised by drug money and intimidated by violent attacks and assasinations. Widely publicized arrests of major Colombian drug traffickers can be meaningless, critics argue, because of the lenient sentences they receive and then serve in relative comfort, while often continuing to manage illicit enterprises.

In Mexico, drug traffickers are believed to have penetrated the former Salinas Administration and may be linked to several political assassinations. Although the current president Ernesto Zedillo, like his predecessor, has pledged to clean up corruption, he may not have sufficient power to do so in the face of the growing influence exercised by traffickers and their bankrolls. One example of the apparent influence of

---

[4] Decertification has potentially severe consequences for a country: the cutoff of U.S. aid (except for narcotics control assistance), U.S. opposition to World Bank and other multilateral development loans to the decertified country, and the stigma of being branded a drug-trafficking nation.

these syndicates with senior police officials occurred in November 1995 when a jet owned by the Cali cartel, loaded with cocaine, landed in the Mexican state of Baja California Sur. Witnesses report that uniformed Mexican Federal Judicial Police unloaded the plane. The cocaine, estimated to be worth $100 million on the U.S. retail market, simply disappeared. In January 1997, a senior Mexican drug prosecutor was assassinated in Tijuana, an event likely prompted by drug-related rivalries among corrupt factions within the state and federal police. On February 6, 1997 Mexican authorities arrested army General Jesus Gutierrez Rebollo, a highly respected career military officer who had been appointed Commissioner of Mexico's National Institute to Combat Drugs in December 1996. Gutierrez and some of his senior staff officers are accused of taking bribes from Mexico's largest drug cartel, the Carrillo Fuentes organization, in return for protecting its operations. Gutierrez' collusion with traffickers is alleged to date from 1990.

INTERNATIONAL DRUG CONTROL: A MULTI-AGENCY FEDERAL EFFORT

Fourteen different Federal departments and agencies are engaged in international drug control efforts. Six principal agencies account for 95 percent of total expenditures: the Customs Service, Department of Defense, Coast Guard, State Department (Bureau for International Narcotics and Law Enforcement Affairs), Drug Enforcement Administration, and the Immigration and Naturalization Service. Information on Central

Intelligence Agency spending is classified, but that agency, like the military today, devotes more of its assets to international drug control intelligence and operations than during the Cold War years. In the past decade, Federal spending on international drug control, including interdiction efforts, reached nearly $20 billion. Approximately 80 percent of that total supported interdiction while 20 percent funded source country programs to reduce drug production and traffic.

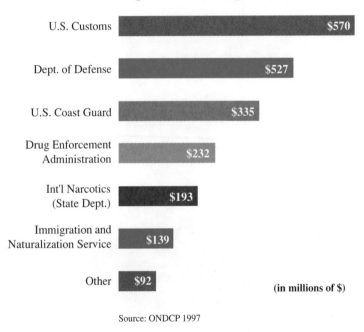

1997 U.S. International Drug Control Budget

U.S. Customs	$570
Dept. of Defense	$527
U.S. Coast Guard	$335
Drug Enforcement Administration	$232
Int'l Narcotics (State Dept.)	$193
Immigration and Naturalization Service	$139
Other	$92

(in millions of $)

Source: ONDCP 1997

U.S. international drug control policy has been nearly synonymous with supply control, primarily through unilateral and bilateral enforcement programs. In addition to unilateral interdiction efforts, American law enforcement agencies work with foreign counterparts in targeting major international drug trafficking organizations. These programs include interdicting drug shipments, arresting traffickers, disrupting transit routes, seizing drug assets and destroying drug processing facilities. Washington also supports source country drug crop eradication programs as well as economic development programs to give farmers alternative livelihoods. A substantial share of U.S. assistance goes to foreign military and police forces to strengthen their drug control capabilities. Reform initiatives to improve the ability of local judicial systems to convict and sentence drug traffickers receive about three percent of

U.S. International
Drug Control Spending 1988-1997

(Total Spending $19.4 billion)

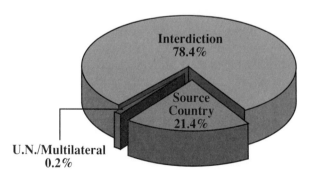

Source: ONDCP 1997
Department of State 1996

total overseas U.S. drug control spending. Latin America has been the primary focus of U.S. international drug control efforts, accounting for 90 percent of total bilateral narcotics assistance since 1981.

The U.S. Government's Annual 'Certification' Process
Despite evidence that distinctions among producer, consumer and transit countries have blurred in recent years, U.S. international drug policy reflects a world view that still divides countries into these categories. This vision underlies the concept of "certification," legislatively imposed upon the Executive Branch by Congress in 1986, which requires the President to determine annually whether the governments of drug producing and transit countries have fully cooperated with the United States in curtailing illicit production and trafficking. Decertification results in the termination of U.S. aid (except for narcotics control assistance), U.S. opposition to multilateral development loans to the decertified country, and the stigma of being branded a drug-trafficking nation.

A "national interest" exception is used to justify waiving the penalties for a country that would otherwise have been decertified—a diplomatic lever to improve performance without actually cutting off assistance. For example, in 1995, Peru, Bolivia, Colombia, Paraguay and Pakistan were certified under national interest exceptions. The *threat* of decertification has been used to try to pressure friendly countries into greater cooperation. However, potential cooperation is often limited by the fact that governments are not able to exert effective control over drug production areas.

The dominance of broader U.S. interests have made the use of decertification, actual or threatened, inconsistent in practice. The United States is less likely to decertify countries where economic, trade and security concerns lead the bilateral agenda. In 1996, after extensive debate within the U.S. government, the United States decided to certify Mexico, but to decertify Colombia (largely because of allegations of illicit campaign contributions involving President Ernesto Samper). Many Latin American leaders and drug control experts criticized this decision, which they believed did not take into account Colombian efforts in 1995, including increased drug seizures, arrests of Cali cartel members, and some drug eradication. The certification process, they noted, harmed relations with both Mexico—which was certified amid intense public controversy—and Colombia—which was not certified—without producing any measurable benefits in terms of narcotics control.[5] Moreover, critics pointed to what they saw as a double standard at work. Colombia's annual trade with the United States is valued at $6 to $7 billion, compared to annual commerce with Mexico of about $80-90 billion. Additionally, Mexico shares a border with the United States, making Mexican cooperation on a range of issues such as crime, immigration and environmental protection essential to Washington.

In addition to apparent inconsistency in application,

---

[5] Decertification of Colombia has had mixed results. Nationalistic reaction to the U.S. decision buoyed President Samper's flagging popularity. However, Samper's government did move forward on drug-related asset seizure legislation long urged by Washington. How that legislation will fare in a judicial system that is often lenient with Colombian traffickers is not clear.

there are two larger problems with the certification process. First, certification implies that the source of America's drug problems is foreign countries that refuse to cooperate. As one Task Force participant asked, "The U.S. is now a major drug producer, but who will certify its anti-narcotics efforts?" (The State Department's *International Narcotics Control Strategy Report* gives estimates of marijuana production for every country except the United States.) Second, the decertification process—by focusing on one aspect of often complex bilateral relationships—can distort the management of U.S. foreign policy. In Latin America, the certification process has been particularly acrimonious and apparently at odds with President Clinton's position that the nations of the Western Hemisphere should look to the United States as a partner in a broader effort to establish a community of democracies.

Actual decertification has been used sparingly. The decertification process's potential political and economic costs make U.S. administrations reluctant to use it, especially in countries where the United States has important strategic interests in addition to drug control. Countries such as Burma, Iran and Syria, where U.S. influence is slight or non-existent, are consistently denied certification. Yet observers point out that Iran pursues a vigorous drug control effort, forcibly eradicating opium crops, seizing large stocks of drugs, arresting users, and executing traffickers. By contrast, Russia is both a substantial opium producer as well as a transit country and money laundering center of growing importance but it is not included on the list of countries requiring annual certification.

Multilateral Initiatives

Three major international treaties form the legal framework for international drug control cooperation: the 1961 Single Convention on Narcotic Drugs; the 1971 Convention on Psychotropic Substances; and the 1988 Convention Against Illicit Traffic in Narcotic Drugs and Psychotropic Substances. Since the Hague Opium Convention of 1912, which pledged nations for the first time to control production and distribution of opium, the United States has taken a leading role in developing multilateral treaties to curtail illicit drug production and trafficking. Indeed, ratification of these treaties is one measure of cooperation that the United States reviews as part of its annual certification process.

U.N. agencies such as the United Nations International Drug Control Program (UNDCP) and the International Narcotics Control Board (INCB) and regional groups such as the Organization of American States (OAS) and the Andean Pact provide important opportunities for developing drug control cooperation through the concept of shared responsibility. International agencies, however, by their very nature rely on persuasion and consensus-building, often a time-consuming process. U.S. support for drug control efforts by multilateral organizations has been modest—on average about five million dollars annually since 1987.

U. N. debates of 15 years ago were generally polarized along traditional consumer/producer lines, with the South insisting that the drug problem was essentially the fault of the North (especially the United States) for failing to address its own demand for drugs. Now U. N. members share a broad consensus that production of narcotics, and not just their use, is part of the problem, and that all countries, including those in the South, are at risk of drug abuse and drug-related violence in their own societies. These changes have fostered a growing sense of shared responsibility for a shared problem.

This principle of shared responsibility formed the basis of the Hemispheric Anti-Drug Strategy ratified by Latin American countries in December 1996, an initiative President Clinton had proposed at the 1994 Miami Summit of the Americas. The principle underlay the December 1995 treaty between the Andean nations and the European Community (EC) on controlling precursor chemicals, the first direct programmatic link between hemispheres on drug control. The EC subsequently negotiated a similar agreement with Mexico, providing another example of how the international community can be active partners in international drug control efforts.

Multilateral organizations provide important fora for addressing drug control problems of interest to the United States. By developing drug control programs on a multilateral basis, member nations can avoid making national sovereignty a domestic political issue, a frequent source of friction accompanying bilateral programs with the United States. This multilateral approach holds particular promise in promoting police and judicial reform and is essential in countering money laundering. The UNDCP, for example, is active in promoting judicial and law enforcement institutions. The Financial Action Task Force (FATF), established by the Group of Seven (G-7) following its 1989 Paris Summit, is a good example of how multilateral initiatives can contribute to international drug control. The FATF, with an expanded membership, has provided the major impetus in strengthening cooperation among industrialized countries to address money laundering. With FATF as an example, the OAS is now considering a Colombian proposal to address money laundering on a cooperative regional basis.

Measuring Success by Operational
Criteria Is Misleading
The United States generally measures the progress of its international drug control initiatives in terms of operational activities: hectares of drug crops eradicated, numbers of drug laboratories destroyed, shipments seized and traffickers arrested. Since 1986, the annual certification of other countries' cooperation with the United States has served as an amalgam of these activity-based indicators. Although the final determination of which countries pass the test and which fail is subject to larger political considerations, the underlying yardstick remains operational.

These activity-based indicators, however, can be misleading. Operating agencies, both in the United States and abroad, know their performance will be judged by these statistical measures and tend to cast their actions and successes accordingly. Activity measures tend to ignore important qualitative distinctions. For example, the destruction of older, less productive coca plants in their declining years is worth less in supply reduction terms than eradication of those just entering their productive phase. That distinction is not reliably made in crop eradication data. From 1987 to 1993, the Bolivian government used $48 million in U.S. aid to pay farmers the equivalent of $2,000 for each destroyed hectare of coca which had been planted more than three years previously. An estimated 26,000 hectares of old coca plants were eliminated. During those same years, Bolivian farmers planted more than 35,000 new hectares of coca, which soon reached much greater productivity than the plants eradicated. The unintended effect of U.S. assistance was to create a coca price stabilization system.

Second, the value of drug seizures in the past has often been expressed in terms of the U.S. retail price, regardless of where the drugs are captured. Most of the drug's value is added after entering the United States due to higher risks of apprehension and punishment and the higher costs of U.S. labor. Assigning U.S. retail costs to seizures made overseas vastly overstates financial losses suffered by traffickers. The closer the seizures are to the point of production, the cheaper the drugs are to replace. (The Task Force is encouraged to note that U.S. agencies are moving away from this practice.)

Third, activity-based measures are open to conflicting interpretations. For example, while larger or more frequent drug seizures might be offered as evidence of success, they may instead reflect increased production and trafficking. Conversely, declining seizures at a given site might also be presented as an indicator of law enforcement effectiveness, but may instead mean that traffickers have shifted their routes.

The apparent logic of relying on interdiction and source-country activities to reduce the supplies of drugs for the U.S. market is compelling—no incoming drugs, no drug problem. (This logic overlooks illegal domestic drug production.) Even if foreign drugs cannot be eliminated entirely, the logic goes, the laws of the marketplace dictate that reducing supplies will drive up price.

That should, in turn, deter potential users from trying drugs and force addicts to seek treatment or stop using on their own. Thus, the price and purity of foreign drugs seized in the United States or at the borders have become accepted benchmarks of progress. If America's overseas drug control initiatives are succeeding (through interdiction, crop eradication, destruction of laboratories and arrests of traffickers), drugs coming into this country should be increasingly expensive and less pure.

Judged by these measures, U.S. strategic efforts to reduce foreign supplies of drugs have not succeeded. Although Federal spending on international drug control has increased fourfold since 1981, drug prices on American streets have declined. In March 1995, DEA Administrator Thomas Constantine testified before Congress that "drug availability and purity of cocaine and heroin are at an all-time high."

As availability and purity have increased, drug prices in the United States have decreased. Worldwide opium production has more than doubled since the early 1980s and now exceeds 4,000 tons a year—the rough equivalent of 400 tons of heroin. Since 1982, heroin's U.S. retail price (per pure gram) has fallen by nearly two-thirds, and its national average purity exceeds 50 precent, compared to only 10 percent 15 years ago. Over the same period, worldwide coca production has also doubled, and cocaine's U.S. retail price (per pure gram) has fallen by two-thirds even as its average retail purity has risen from 47 to 70 percent. This increase in domestic availability of low cost, high purity drugs has come despite numerous tactical successes by U.S. and cooperating foreign law enforcement authorities, who estimate that they interdict about one-third of the cocaine destined for the United States.

Cocaine Prices Dropping Despite U.S. International Drug Control Spending

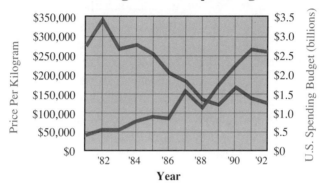

Source: DEA Illegal Drug Price/Purity Reports

MONEY LAUNDERING: HIDING DRUG PROFITS

Money laundering[6] is indispensable for putting drug profits to use. Sophisticated groups like the Colombian cartels take advantage of the weakest links in the global regulatory system by shifting transactions, communications and assets to countries with the weakest or most corruptible authorities, the most restrictive bank secrecy, extradition, or asset seizure

---

[6] Money laundering is the process whereby illegal profits are maneuvered through the financial system to conceal their source, confuse the money trail and return them to the owner, legitimized and ready for use. The process can be broken down into three distinct phases: "placement" of the "dirty" money in a financial institution or purchase of an asset; "layering" to disguise the source of funds by distributing them among other institutions as investments; and "integration" into the legitimate financial and economic system.

laws, and the most ineffective bank supervision. It is estimated that drug traffickers pay commissions ranging from 15 to 25 percent for money laundering services. Within the last decade, targeting major drug assets has become an important focus of U.S. drug control strategy.

As recently as the early 1980s, an anti-money laundering framework was lacking in most countries and was totally absent at the international level. Although the 1970 U.S. Bank Secrecy Act addressed money laundering, it was not criminalized in the United States until the 1986 Money Laundering Control Act. The 1988 Convention Against Illicit Traffic in Narcotic Drugs and Psychotropic Substances was a major step in enlisting the global community in a multilateral initiative against drug trafficking. The Convention requires signatory governments to criminalize drug-related money laundering; to assert their legal authority to confiscate criminal profits; and to exclude bank secrecy as grounds for declining to act against money laundering. The 1988 Convention has been ratified by more than 100 governments.

The G-7 decided in 1989 to create the Financial Action Task Force (FATF) to harmonize global money laundering controls. The FATF produced 40 recommendations on measures to control money laundering through financial institutions and to improve international cooperation in money laundering investigations. The European Union passed a 1991 Directive on money laundering controls (patterned after the FATF recommendations) that EU member countries are required to incorporate into their domestic laws. The 1994 Summit of the Americas included commitments to coordinate a hemispheric response to combat money laundering.

Effective implementation of these agreements has thus far eluded the international community, in part because money laundering specialists use state-of-the-art methods to stay well ahead of law enforcement. A second problem is the huge volume of international financial transactions. In the United States alone, more than a trillion dollars move in and out of the financial system daily. Hiding illicit transfers in that flow is being made easier with the growing use of cybercurrency (electronic money) systems using on-line encryption devices. Additionally, there are difficult social, political and legal challenges inherent in imposing a strict financial reporting regime on capital flows in democratic societies where expanding international trade, economic development and prosperity are believed to depend upon the free flow of global capital. Control regimes construed as hindering that capital flow get even less support in countries with traditions of bank secrecy, whether to protect non-drug related flight capital or, as with many offshore banking havens, simply as a means of attracting new money.

There is no official accounting of the resources dedicated to money laundering controls by the numerous U.S. agencies involved.[7] The best guess of one veteran IRS agent is around $400 million per year, making no distinction between domestic and international operations and programs. Apart from the large

---

[7] Federal agencies for money laundering enforcement and/or prevention include: Department of State, Customs Service, Internal Revenue Service, Federal Bureau of Investigtions, Financial Crimes Enforcement Network (FinCEN) and the Postal Service.

flows of legitimate money transfers in which to hide drug profits, the advantage remains with the criminals. Uneven legislation among the world's governments, 'offshore' banking safe havens and the speed and ease of electronic commerce make enforcement difficult. Experience in the United States, the world's largest economy and most lucrative drug market, suggests that not all of the enforcement challenges lie abroad. According to DEA estimates, three-quarters of Colombian drug proceeds are laundered through New York City. Moreover, according to the State Department's 1996 International Narcotics Control Status Report, "U.S. financial systems continue to be exploited, at levels probably not approached by any other country."

U.S. SOURCE COUNTRY PROGRAMS: UNINTENDED EFFECTS

U.S. drug control initiatives have had unintended adverse consequences, particularly in Latin America, the primary focus of U.S. drug control funding for the past two decades. Eradication campaigns stir political unrest and violence among farmers who depend upon drug crops as their principal source of income. Peru's president Alberto Fujimori's stance offers an example of how domestic realities affect foreign political leaders, even those who otherwise cooperate closely with U.S. anti-drug efforts. Fujimori has endorsed the U.S.-financed Operation Laser Strike to intercept planes smuggling coca paste and cocaine from Peru to Colombia. Fujimori, however, has refused to approve large-scale coca eradication until viable economic alternatives are provided for coca growers. (The Shining Path insurgency, which paralyzed the country for almost a decade, drew some of its strength from disaffected coca farmers.) Since 1993, estimated Peruvian coca leaf production increased 20 percent, which accounts for 60 percent of the world's total.

In Bolivia, U.S.-funded eradication operations have consistently drawn strong opposition from well-organized coca farmers, who comprise about 10 percent of the country's agricultural work force. Faced with the threat of decertification and the cut-off of $81 million in annual foreign aid from the United States, the Bolivian government in 1995 resumed coca eradication efforts, despite demonstrations by farmers which the police forcibly suppressed. Although the government claimed a 5 percent reduction in potentially harvestable coca leaf tonnage, additional plantings increased slightly the overall area under cultivation. Bolivia continues to produce approximately one-fourth of the world's coca leaf, the third largest producer behind Peru and Colombia (which now grows slightly more than Bolivia).

In Colombia, U.S.-supported drug eradication efforts have had limited results. In 1995, the Colombian military undertook a vigorous coca eradication program. Coca farmers in southern Colombia staged protests alleging government failure to keep previous agreements to provide economic development for the region. Instead, they complained, the Colombian military was depopulating the area and destroying food crops by herbicidal spraying. In the end, government forces reported destroying nearly

9,000 hectares of coca (and no opium). Nevertheless, new plantings increased Colombia's total coca cultivation by 14 percent, to 50,900 hectares in 1995.

In the United States, local opposition has impeded Federal and state enforcement efforts to eradicate illicit marijuana cultivation in California, Oregon and other states. In November 1996, voters in California and Arizona approved state legislation permitting doctors to prescribe marijuana for medical purposes, which conflicts with Federal law. The courts have not yet clarified whether the new state laws permit marijuana cultivation for personal medical use.

U.S. International Drug Control Efforts Can Hinder Development of Stable Democracies
Drug crops are usually grown in remote areas where civilian government exercises limited authority, especially when anti-government insurgencies are present which rely on drug production and traffic for financial support. In pursuing crop eradication, the United States often has had little practical alternative to working with host country armed forces rather than police forces that may be under-trained, under-equipped and corrupt. Critics note that the United States is thereby 'militarizing' the drug war at a time when many Latin American countries are working to consolidate fragile democracies after decades of military rule.

Beginning with the 1989 Andean Initiative, the U.S. has urged Latin American governments to involve their armed forces in drug control. At the time, Andean governments insisted that more attention be paid to the economic aspects of drug production and resisted the full-blown military role advocated by the

United States, citing many of the same reasons why the U.S. military has traditionally been precluded from domestic law enforcement. Nevertheless, the Andean countries eventually agreed to greater participation by their armed forces. One result has been to validate a new internal security role for Latin American militaries, further blurring the distinction between civilian and military responsibilities.

U.S. Drug Control Assistance to the Andes 1989-1996

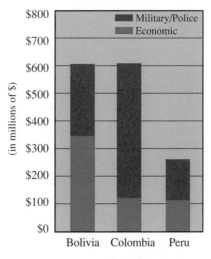

Source: AID Congressional
Presentation 1990-1997

An enhanced military role in drug control also increases the potential for corruption. Although corruption plagues enforcement efforts regardless of the institution, the military's power and traditional lack of accountability magnify this problem. As one Latin

American expert told the Task Force, "For the sake of legitimate ends [drug control], U.S. policy relies on the most anti-democratic, corrupt and unaccountable forces in Latin America. The U.S. is looking for a short-cut to drug control by using these institutions, and letting one issue dominate all others."

The presence of insurgencies further complicates the drug control picture in Latin America. For example, the Colombian military has at times pursued counterinsurgency—its top priority—through *de facto* alliances with private paramilitary organizations and other groups reportedly involved in the drug traffic. The Colombian government is now seeking to restore the army's power to conduct judicial investigations, something it lost 15 years ago, as the country strengthened its democratic institutions. Charging military units with drug enforcement responsibilities can exacerbate problems of corruption, which has been noted as a recurring problem in Bolivia and other Latin American countries by the State Department's annual *International Narcotics Control Strategy Report*. Gonzalo Sanchez de Losada, former Planning Minister and current President of Bolivia, described the threat posed by an unaccountable military when he said "When you have a corrupt chief of police, you fire him. When you have a corrupt chief of the army, he fires you."

In Venezuela, the head of the National Guard's anti-drug bureau from 1987 to 1991 was recently indicted by a U.S. grand jury for smuggling 22 tons of cocaine into the United States. during his tenure, a period when he worked closely with the DEA and CIA. In Peru, hundreds of pounds of cocaine were seized in 1996 on Peruvian Navy ships and Air Force planes. In Mexico, the Federal Judicial Police (MFJP), the lead drug enforcement agency for the past 25 years, has a long history of corruption. As the first step in a major judicial reform effort, former Mexican Attorney General Antonio Lozano fired 737 police officials in September 1996. Lozano's successor, Jorge Madrazo P. Cuellar (Mexico's seventh attorney general in eight years) has pledged to continue the reforms. On February 21, 1997, Madrazo removed 87 MFJP officers in Baja California Norte along the western U.S.-Mexico border where Mexican officials acknowledge the Tijuana cartel has corrupted federal and state enforcement agencies. The police officers were replaced by 46 army soldiers. This action followed the government's revelation two days earlier that military General Jesus Gutierrez Rebollo, Mexico's top drug enforcement official and some of his senior staff had been arrested on charges of taking bribes from major drug dealers.

Human Rights Abuses and Drug Control
The protection of human rights and the strengthening of democratic institutions are important U.S. foreign policy objectives. U.S. international drug control programs in source countries have at times come into conflict with those objectives. It is important to remember that human rights abuses in Latin American and other countries are not new; nor will they disappear if the United States withdraws support for source country drug control activities. Every effort should be made, however, to ensure that U.S. drug control policy and programs do not contribute to human rights problems.

U.S.-provided equipment is not always used for the drug control purposes specified in the agreements under which it is given. Recent General Accounting Office (GAO) reports conclude that despite bilateral agreements governing the use of equipment, the U.S. cannot effectively monitor the 'end-use' of its anti-narcotics enforcement assistance. The State Department concedes that it generally must rely on reporting from recipient governments for that purpose.

Since 1989 the United States has provided the Colombian armed forces and police with more than $500 million in drug control equipment, including helicopters, utility vehicles, planes, and weapons. A recent report prepared by U.S. military personnel in Colombia found that in 1992 and 1993 a large share of drug control equipment that went to army units heavily involved in counter-insurgency activity was commingled with counter-insurgency equipment. Although this reflects the Colombian government's view that guerrillas and drug traffickers are not easily distinguishable, commingling U.S.-provided equipment may violate legal restrictions governing proper use of U.S. assistance. Plans by the U.S. Department of Defense to work with Peruvian military forces in a riverine drug interdiction program raise similar problems. A State Department official acknowledged in the February 3, 1997 *New York Times* the difficulties of sorting out drug control activities from counter-insurgency, noting that "...you still have to deal with the insurgency at night. What you are talking about is imposing control over areas that the central Government has never controlled."

In 1997, the United States plans to provide Colombia with $25 million in anti-narcotics equipment and support for the military and police, despite confirmed human rights abuses. According to the State

Department's Human Rights Report for 1996, the Colombian government's overall human rights record remained poor: "Although extrajudicial killings by the security force declined somewhat, the armed forces and the police continued to be responsible for serious abuses including, according to credible reports, instances of death squad activity within the army."

In Mexico, the military used helicopters purchased with U.S. drug control aid to transport troops to the southern state of Chiapas to fight guerrillas in 1994. Meanwhile, a 1996 GAO report found that "U.S. and Mexican efforts have had little, if any, impact on the overall flow of drugs through Mexico into the U.S."

Looking at the interplay between human rights and commingling of drug control funding with counter-insurgency efforts in Latin America, one Task Force member who served as U.S. ambassador to several countries in that region observed, "Based upon my experience in the region, nothing is working against drugs, including the military strategy. We won't see real improvements before there is an effective transition to democratic, accountable, market-oriented states."

Charges of human rights violations have also been directed at the actions of special U.S.-funded anti-drug units in Bolivia, which have received more than $250 million in U.S. military and police aid since 1989. U.S. assistance supports about two-thirds of the salaries and 90 percent of the operating expenses of the anti-drug police known as UMOPAR. Human rights monitors allege that UMOPAR has routinely conducted arbitrary mass searches, arrests, thefts, and beatings of coca growers in the Chapare Valley, where most of Bolivia's coca is grown.

In Latin American societies, judicial institution building is an important objective of national governments as well as U.S. international drug policy. By reforming the courts which hear drug-related cases, policy makers hoped to see more traffickers convicted. However, human rights groups note that even the U.S.-supported Rule of Law (ROL) program to strengthen Andean judiciaries may be doing more harm than good. In Colombia and Bolivia, the ROL program supports special anti-drug legislation and courts which often violate fundamental due process guarantees without speeding up drug trials and convictions—their intended goal. Because of corruption within the judicial system, poor detainees remain in jail for years awaiting trial while drug traffickers pay bribes to obtain release or plea bargain for shorter sentences.

THE LIMITS TO INTERNATIONAL SUPPLY CONTROL

The downward trend of drug prices indicates a general failure of U.S. international drug control policy to meet its goals, notwithstanding the increased profile and resources accorded interdiction and source-country programs since the early 1980s. In the absence of international supply control efforts, domestic drug prices might have fallen to even lower levels. But the goal of raising prices high enough to keep drugs out of reach for most consumers is still remote. The key question for policy makers is whether the evident lack of success to date stems from inadequate implementation of an otherwise sound policy or whether the poor results reflect more fundamental strategic flaws. Policy makers have not in the past questioned whether the strategy is appropriate, arguing instead that success simply requires more resources, more time, and better coordination.

Different Administrations and Congresses have emphasized different tactics, arguably to the detriment of program continuity. For example, President Reagan emphasized border interdiction, while President Clinton has stressed source country efforts. Drug control is also one of several U.S. policy objectives in any country (which may be less than fully compatible with each other). Lack of coordination among both U.S. agencies and national governments is a long-standing, serious problem. Moreover, in the present climate of budget austerity, interdiction and source country programs may face future funding constraints or, at the very least, level budgets.

The Task Force's analysis suggests that while operational problems—faulty coordination, lack of continuity, and resource constraints—may contribute to the policy's poor record, they are not decisive, even when taken together. As described below, certain basic obstacles severely limit the potential of international supply-control initiatives to reduce U.S. drug problems.

The Economics of Drug Cultivation
Drug crops can be grown cheaply almost anywhere in the world, and farmers have strong economic incentives to shift, expand or modify cultivation as required to protect their livelihoods. Enforcement directed at growers tends to disperse cultivation to ever more remote areas, making detection and eradication even

more difficult. In Peru and Bolivia, for example, only one percent of land suitable for coca is now being cultivated, leaving vast areas for growers to use if their current fields are targeted by eradication efforts.

Sustained eradication requires viable economic alternatives for drug crop farmers. The only example of prolonged, significant reductions in drug production in the past two decades is Thailand, where rapid economic growth created real alternatives for opium farmers. Additionally, favorable political and security conditions permitted Thai authorities to carry out limited eradication while international development agencies as well as the United States supplied substantial development programs in the growing areas.

Placing the accomplishments of U.S. anti-drug programs in the context of overall production trends provides a better sense of program impact. The State Department reports that eradication programs from 1989 through 1995 eliminated about 55,000 hectares of Andean coca, enough to have produced about 270 metric tons of cocaine. However, over this six-year period, net coca cultivation after eradication in those same Andean countries was still an estimated 1.45 million hectares, equivalent to about 7,250 metric tons of cocaine. As General McCaffrey, Director of the Office of National Drug Control Policy, concluded in a January 23, 1997 interview with National Public Radio, "If we look back on the last six years in Peru, we've made absolutely no progress reducing the acreage under coca cultivation until this last year when we appear to see President Fujimori's energies starting to bear fruit. But essentially, production's been level for six years. Bolivia...production's gone up for six

Worldwide Opium and Coca
Production, 1984-1995

Opium

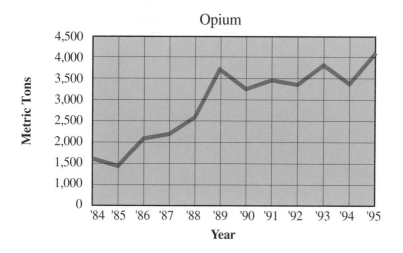

Coca

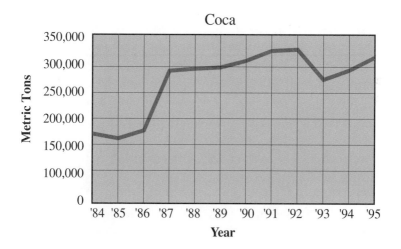

Sources: Department of State INCSR 1987-1996

years. Production of opium in Colombia's gone from zero to sixty-five metric tons a year...So, it's sort of a discouraging situation."

The Price Structure of the Drug Market
Interdiction continues to achieve impressive tactical successes against drug traffickers, but these efforts have been overwhelmed by the volume of drug production. Drugs are now so plentiful that even the largest seizures have little impact on drug availability in the United States. Traffickers quickly move on to new sources, shipments and routes.

Intensive U.S. interdiction efforts in the Caribbean in the 1980s effectively turned Mexico into a major transit zone by forcing Colombian traffickers into alternative routes. In recent months, the eastern Pacific has become a major maritime route for South American drugs bound for the United States. The U.S.-assisted Peruvian and Colombian campaign to intercept cocaine flights brought down 39 planes in 1995, but only a few in 1996. Avoiding the more dangerous air routes, traffickers have shifted to river routes through dense, sparsely populated jungles which makes detection far more difficult. The U.S. Department of Defense is now studying ways to assist Peruvian forces in a major riverine interdiction effort. If, and when, these river routes become too risky, the traffickers will move on to other areas.

The largest drug profits are made within the United States at the level of street sales, not in foreign poppy or coca fields or on the high seas. The total cost of cultivating, refining and smuggling cocaine to the United States accounts for less than 15 percent of retail prices here. Recent anecdotal evidence from the Southwestern border of the United States suggests that smuggling costs may now be higher, as Mexican traffickers are said to be offering as much as half their cocaine shipments in exchange for safe passage. Still, the value of the drugs at that point in the transit process remains only a fraction of the price at the retail level on American streets. As one DEA official explained, "The average drug organization can afford to lose as much as 80 percent of its product and still be profitable." Street level enforcement in the United States has proved the most effective way of raising retail prices for illicit drugs; through a greater police presence, it also helps deter violence generated by street drug markets.

U.S. Consumes a Small Portion of
Worldwide Drug Production
According to the DEA, Americans used 10 metric tons of heroin in 1995, less than 3 percent of potential worldwide production (for 1995, more than 400 metric tons) based upon current opium yield estimates. Our nearly 300 ton annual cocaine consumption represents only about one-third of estimated worldwide production potential (for 1995, 780 metric tons). A poppy field of about 30 square miles can supply the American heroin market for a year while cocaine demand can be met from coca fields of about 300 square miles. Americans consume a small amount of the estimated worldwide production of marijuana (for 1995, 7,839 metric tons, not including U.S. production for which there is no official U.S. estimate). Recognizing that illicit drug imports constitute a minute fraction of the

Prices of Cocaine Through
the Distribution System
(per pure kilo equivalent)

Chicago
Retail
$188,000

Miami
Import $23,000

Colombia
Export
$1,050

Peru
Leaf $650

Source: CIA State Department
Conference Report, 1994

annual commerce across U.S. borders puts the difficult task of interdiction in perspective: each year an estimated 436 million people enter the United States by land, sea and air; 116 million motor vehicles cross U.S. borders; and more than 9 million shipping containers and 400 million tons of cargo enter U.S. ports.

Limits to Price as Drug Policy Tool
A key goal of international drug control efforts is to make drugs more expensive in the United States in order to reduce drug abuse. However, only very steep price increases are likely to curtail drug consumption among heavy drug users and addicts. Sufficiently steep price increases appear unlikely based upon the experience of the past two decades.

Task Force members noted that even if higher drug prices could be achieved, they would stimulate increased drug-related crime as addicts seek additional money to buy more expensive drugs. The importance of heavy users' demand for drugs is underscored by the changing composition of America's cocaine-using population. After peaking in the early 1980s, the number of cocaine users has declined by half, but the overall quantity of cocaine consumed annually has remained high. Increased cocaine use by addicts has compensated for the decreased number of "light" users. In 1992, two-thirds of total cocaine consumption in this country was attributed to "heavy" users most resistant to price changes, who constitute only one-fifth of all American cocaine users.

Raising the price for domestic users can also raise profits for traffickers. Because most of the costs of illicit drugs are added once they are in the United

States, a trafficker's overhead outside this country is relatively low. When U.S. retail prices go up, traffickers can increase short-term profits by increasing supplies destined to the U.S. market.

International drug control efforts do not reduce illicit drug cultivation and production within the United States. As noted earlier, marijuana is produced in the United States, as are illicit synthetic drugs: methamphetamine, lysergic acid diethylamide (LSD), PCP and the hallucinogen MDMA (ecstacy). Abuse of these synthetics, while small in comparison with cocaine, heroin and marijuana abuse, is growing modestly. These drugs are potential substitutes if foreign drugs become unavailable. According to the United Nations' International Narcotics Control Board, clandestine manufacture in the United States of methamphetamine is increasing, and U.S.-based LSD laboratories supply drug markets in Europe as well as the United States.

REDUCING THE DEMAND FOR DRUGS: KEY TO LASTING PROGRESS

During the 1970s, U.S. international drug control efforts were linked closely to domestic demand reduction. In the face of a nationwide heroin epidemic, President Richard Nixon established the Special Action Office of Drug Abuse Prevention (SAODAP) in 1971 to supervise all Federal prevention, treatment and research programs. Between 1970 and 1975, prevention, education and treatment received nearly two-thirds of the total Federal drug budget—$1.92 billion out of $3 billion. Under Presidents Ford and Carter,

Federal drug policy moved toward enforcement, which received about half of all funding from 1976 to 1981. By the end of the 1970s, the spread of heroin addiction had been contained. The number of addicts declined from an estimated 800,000 to 500,000, a number which remained relatively constant throughout the 1980s.

Declaring an all-out "war on drugs," President Reagan radically changed the focus of Federal drug funding, concentrating on law enforcement and interdiction over demand reduction. Funding for drug enforcement more than doubled from $800 million in 1981 to $1.9 billion in 1985. During the same period, Federal support for prevention, education and treatment declined from $404 million to $338 million. Subsequent Administrations have continued to emphasize law enforcement over demand reduction. In 1997, one-third of the Federal budget funding supports prevention, education and treatment, while two-thirds supports interdiction, enforcement, and international supply reduction efforts.

Much of the progress against drug abuse in the past decade comes from reduced demand, which has declined in the face of increasing supplies of ever cheaper drugs. Between 1986 and 1992, marijuana and cocaine use dropped by half, reflecting the power of health concerns and negative social attitudes towards drugs (which sharpened after the sudden cocaine overdose death of sports star Len Bias in 1986). The "Just Say No" campaign, led by Mrs. Nancy Reagan during the 1980s, also contributed to social disapproval of drug use. The recent increase in teen drug use (which has doubled since 1992) suggests that public perceptions of the risks of drug use have changed and social attitudes have become more tolerant. These trends are reported in annual nationwide surveys of junior high, high school and college students. Reversing this pattern will require expanded prevention and education efforts that build on the research of the past decade.

Extensive research shows that school prevention programs can reduce new drug use by half and new alcohol use by a third among early adolescents. These programs, built on social learning theory, teach children to recognize the internal and external pressures which influence them to smoke, drink, and use drugs. They also learn how to resist these pressures through role-playing in the classroom. The cost of these programs ranges from $15 to $25 per pupil, including classroom materials and teacher training. Program effects are stronger when prevention includes families, media, and the community in a comprehensive effort to discourage alcohol, tobacco, and drug use. Advertising by the Partnership for a Drug-Free America has accelerated negative attitudes towards illegal drugs among some groups, particularly in markets where their ads appear frequently.

Treatment has also proved effective in reducing drug use and drug crime. National studies that have followed tens of thousands of addicts through different kinds of programs report that the single most important factor is length of time in treatment. One-third of those who stay in treatment longer than three months are drug-free a year after leaving treatment. The success rate jumps to two-thirds when treatment lasts a year or longer. And programs that provide intensive, highly structured treatment with supportive follow-up services (like vocational education, job training, and housing referral) report even better results.

Treatment is far less expensive than the alternatives. An untreated addict can cost society an estimated $43,200 annually, compared with an average $18,000 for a year of residential treatment or $2,000 in an outpatient program. A 1994 statewide study in California found that $1 invested in alcohol and drug treatment saved taxpayers $7.14 in future costs. Drug courts, which divert nonviolent offenders from prison to court-supervised drug treatment, are also cost-effective: studies report that drug courts cut recidivism by half among treated offenders at a small fraction of the cost of incarceration (about $30,000 a year on average).

Treatment is also more cost-effective than international supply reduction efforts. A 1994 RAND study found that $34 million invested in treatment reduced cocaine use as much as $783 million spent for foreign source country programs or $366 million for interdiction.

Treatment Is Cost-Effective

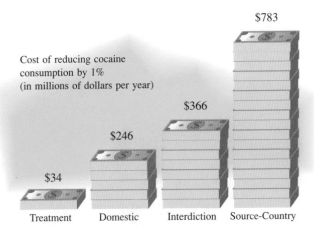

Cost of reducing cocaine
consumption by 1%
(in millions of dollars per year)

$783

$366

$246

$34

Treatment   Domestic   Interdiction   Source-Country

Source: RAND Drug Policy Research Center

Community law enforcement plays an important role in reducing demand: cleaning up street drug markets makes neighborhoods safer by protecting residents from violence and drug dealing. As the recent success of New York City's "broken windows" enforcement campaign attests, safer neighborhoods produce many benefits, including reductions in crime and greater citizen involvement in community life. Community level enforcement also sends an important social message that drug dealing will not be tolerated, reinforcing community and school prevention efforts.

SUMMARY

Since 1981, the U.S. government has spent more than $25 billion for foreign interdiction and source country programs intended to reduce the supplies of drugs coming into this country. Despite impressive seizures at the border, on the high seas, and in other countries, foreign drugs are cheaper and more readily available in the United States today than two decades ago. Domestic production of illegal drugs is increasing, suggesting that American sources could potentially meet future foreign shortfalls, if any occur. Moreover, these programs have created problems of their own, strained relations with other countries, particularly in Latin America; political unrest among peasant farmers who rely on drug crops for their livelihood; human rights abuses as governments try to suppress drug cultivation; increased corruption among police and military forces; and expanding roles for the military in drug enforcement and internal security in countries where democracy is still fragile.

The Task Force believes that America's international drug control priorities should shift from a primary focus on foreign drug supplies to the growing power and profits of the transnational drug cartels that challenge the integrity of political, financial and judicial institutions in this country and abroad. The United States should place greater emphasis on efforts both to strengthen democratic governments and to combat money-laundering, drug-related corruption and violence through bilateral and multilateral initiatives. The

Task Force also believes that international efforts, however successful, cannot be expected to reduce drug abuse within this country. Demand reduction—prevention, education, treatment, community law enforcement—is key in achieving sustained progress in addressing America's drug problems.

ADDITIONAL AND
DISSENTING VIEWS

Task Force member Sergio Galvis endorses the overall conclusion of the report that continuing supply-side control measures should be complemented by further and more effective demand-reduction policies. In that connection, he considers it significant that, as the report notes, between 1986 and 1992 negative social attitudes toward illegal drugs contributed to a 50 percent reduction in the numbers of Americans who used marijuana and cocaine. He does not agree, however, with the implication in the report that supply-side control policies, which rely in part on military action against drug-producing and trafficking organizations, inevitably hinder democratic development in producing and exporting countries and contribute to human rights abuses. In Mr. Galvis' view, in certain countries where the nexus between illegal narcotics activities and insurgency groups is growing, effective and responsible action by local professional military forces, combined with international support through education and materiel, can play a critical role in protecting democratic institutions and improving social conditions.

Sergio Galvis

Task Force member Peter Hakim considered it questionable whether a group with primary expertise in foreign relations should focus its recommendations on U.S. domestic drug control policy. He agreed that U.S. policy should emphasize the strengthening of democratic institutions to withstand drug-related violence and corruption, and thought that the report would have been more useful if it had offered concrete guidance on how this could be accomplished.

Peter Hakim

I have decided that it would be a mistake and misleading for me to support or be associated with the report or try to deal with my objections in footnotes. Certainly there is material in the report with which I agree. But the report taken as a whole is so negative in substance and tone about United States efforts to stem drug use, production and distribution that it amounts to an invitation to drop those efforts and concentrate on 'demand reduction.' The anti-drug war depends on law enforcement, interdiction, supply reduction, drug use reduction, education and therapy. Turning away from any of these efforts would result in serious damage to the anti-drug movement. The report also makes it seem almost as if the human rights problems in the areas discussed are the fault of the United States anti-drug work. The fact that human rights abuses in these countries are largely the result of their governments, their police, the corruption within, is mentioned only glancingly, almost as a technicality. This is a distortion of historic and current reality that does disservice both to the drug war, and to the cause of human rights.

A.M. Rosenthal

Although Mr. Rosenthal participated in the Task Force, he did not wish to be associated with the Task Force Report. Mr. Rosenthal, a columnist for The New

York Times, *was a foreign correspondent for* the Times *at the United Nations for nine years and later became the Executive Editor. Mr. Rosenthal won the Pulitzer Prize for his work in Poland.*

DISCUSSIONS AT MEETINGS IN FOUR CITIES, OCTOBER — NOVEMBER, 1996

The summaries are intended to convey the broad sense of meeting discussions; they do not in any way represent endorsement of policy recommendations by the listed participants. Institutional affiliations are provided for identification purposes only.

LOS ANGELES, CALIFORNIA OCTOBER 10, 1996

Host:	Abraham F. Lowenthal, *Pacific Council on International Policy*
Comments:	Mathea Falco, *Drug Strategies*
	Miguel Ruiz-Cabañas, *Mexican Foreign Ministry*
	Peter H. Smith, *University of California, San Diego*

In addition to discussing the broad findings of the Task Force, Los Angeles participants provided a unique perspective on the importance of border enforcement efforts. Several members noted that drug interdiction at the border can increase costs to traffickers: recent press stories in California report that Mexican drug cartels take as much as half the Colombian drug shipments they deliver to the United States as payment for their services. (Nonetheless, drug prices within the

United States remain at all-time lows, in part because production continues to expand.) In addition, improved border enforcement sends an important message that the United States is serious about attacking drug crime and cross-border violence. The group agreed that U.S. border efforts should be closely coordinated with Mexico, perhaps through the creation of a special bilateral border commission composed of government officials as well as private citizens. The destabilizing of key countries by drug cartels makes the drug problem a critically important foreign policy issue. However, the group was hesitant to suggest expanded multilateral enforcement strategies, particularly in light of the recent rejection by a summit of Latin American defense ministers of closer anti-drug cooperation with the United States. The group noted the importance of disrupting money laundering networks, seizing drug assets, and stemming the flow of precursor chemicals used in illicit synthetic drug production in this country.

Participants agreed that U.S. concentration on source-country crop eradication and crop substitution programs has been futile, and that even if these efforts could succeed, domestic drug production within the United States would quickly compensate for any shortfalls. From the Mexican perspective, illegal drug cultivation in the United States combined with rising teenage drug abuse raises questions about the sincerity of the U.S. government's commitment to drug control. The group concurred that U.S. foreign policy interests lie in reinforcing democratic governments, strengthening judicial and banking systems, and helping develop professional law enforcement capabilities, particularly in this hemisphere. These U.S. interests are especially prominent in neighboring Mexico, where narco-violence, assassination, and corruption threaten the security of both countries. The Mexican cartels are now so affluent that they spend a reported $500 million a year in bribing officials—an amount double the annual budget of the Mexican Attorney General's office, which has primary responsibility for drug enforcement.

The group concluded that much more needs to be done to reduce the demand for drugs in the United States, which one participant observed would require a "Copernican change" in traditional policy thinking.

LOS ANGELES
MEETING PARTICIPANTS

Peter Andreas, *University of California, San Diego*

Douglas Anglin, *University of California, Los Angeles*

Ramon Bahamonde, *Pacific Council on International Policy*

Gregory Berg, *Los Angeles Police Department*

Alan D. Bersin, *U.S. Attorney for the Southern District of California*

Robert Bonner, *Gibson, Dunn & Crutcher*

Mark E. Buchman, *financial consultant*

Dan Caldwell, *Pepperdine University*

Emma Cherniavsky, *Pacific Council on International Policy*

Thomas Cowley, *Kroll Associates*

Eduardo Martinez Curiel, *Pacific Council on International Policy*

Richarde Drobnick, *University of Southern California*
Susan Everingham, *RAND*
Mathea Falco, *Drug Strategies*
Mike Farrell, *Human Rights Watch-California*
Rodolfo O. de la Garza, *University of Texas at Austin*
Arthur Golden, *San Diego Union-Tribune*
Susan Golding, *Mayor of San Diego*
Michael D. Intriligator, *University of California, Los Angeles*
Jane Jaquette, *Occidental College*
Kristin Johnson, *Pacific Council on International Policy*
David Karl, *Pacific Council on International Policy*
Abraham F. Lowenthal, *Pacific Council on International Policy*
Daniel C. Lynch, *Pacific Council on International Policy*
Vilma S. Martinez, *Munger, Tolles & Olson*
James W. McGuire, *Pacific Council on International Policy*
Kristin McKissick, *Pacific Council on International Policy*
Michael M. Murtaugh, *AT&T*
Catherine O'Neill, *Women's Commission for Refugee Women and Children*
Michael B. Preston, *University of Southern California*
David Richards, *private investor*
Miguel Ruiz-Cabañas, *Mexican Foreign Ministry*
Peter Rydell, *RAND*
Robert Scheer, *Los Angeles Times*
Stanley Sheinbaum, *New Perspectives Quarterly*
Richard M. Sloan, *Southern California Edison Co.*

Peter H. Smith, *University of California, San Diego*
David Sternlight, *U.S./Costa Rica Presidential Advisory Commission*
Gerald L. Warren, *Pacific Council on International Policy*
Michael Woo, *Corporation for National Service*
Adrian Woolridge, *The Economist*

CHICAGO, ILLINOIS
OCTOBER 24, 1996

Host: Adele Simmons, *The John D. and Catherine T. MacArthur Foundation*

Comments: Mathea Falco, *Drug Strategies*

               Miguel Ruiz-Cabañas, *Mexican Foreign Ministry*

The Chicago participants agreed that curtailing U.S. drug consumption requires placing priority on demand reduction. Supply control efforts are important, but the goals of supply control must be clear, and its limits kept in mind. Even if illegal drug imports could be eliminated entirely, the U.S. drug problem would continue, as demand is displaced to other drugs produced domestically. At the same time, traffickers cannot have a free hand; coordinated international efforts must pressure traffickers at the highest levels. However, declining drug prices and rising purity over the past 15 years suggest that international supply-control programs cannot achieve much if demand for drugs continues apace.

The U.S. market for illegal drugs, an enormous problem in its own right, also poses a threat to other countries by enriching criminal organizations. Mexico's president has declared drugs a major national security threat, as traffickers use violence and corruption to subvert political, judicial, and financial institutions. The transnational reach of the major trafficking organizations requires a coordinated international response. From the Mexican perspective, the United States often does not seem committed to drug control, since demand reduction remains a lower priority and illicit marijuana production is expanding. The United States should understand the unique contribution it can make by reducing domestic drug use.

One participant reported that Sweden and other European countries are facing growing addiction problems, supplied by drugs coming in from the former Communist countries. Compared to the United States, however, Sweden places much higher priority on prevention and treatment, which receive about two-thirds of total anti-drug funding. Drug prevention and treatment programs have been shown to be far more cost-effective than international supply control programs in reducing drug abuse. But the U.S. policy debate remains driven by politicians' fear of being labeled "soft" on drugs. The problem is that "tough" sounding approaches—like overseas drug interdiction and eradication campaigns—make for safe politics but dubious policy. As several participants pointed out, a focus on enforcement without due attention to the underlying social pressures and attitudes that foster drug use is a recipe for frustration. U.S. policy should place greater emphasis on prevention and treatment, and should be conceived as a long-term endeavor, not something to be achieved before the next election. A balanced, long-term approach will not "solve" the drug problem, but it will make it more manageable.

CHICAGO MEETING PARTICIPANTS

Patricia Abrams, *Center for Neighborhood Technology*
Kennette Benedict, *MacArthur Foundation*
Peter Bensinger, *Bensinger, DuPont & Associates*
Kelvy Brown, *Mayor of Chicago's Office on Substance Abuse*
Dorothy Burge, *Associated Colleges of the Midwest*
Ingrid and Ingvar Carlsson, *Reed College*
Douglass Cassel, Jr., *DePaul University*
Barbara Cimaglio, *State of Illinois Department of Alcoholism & Substance Abuse*
John Cooper, *University of Wisconsin*
Marcia Dam
Mathea Falco, *Drug Strategies*
Augustin S. Hart, Jr., *retired Vice-Chairman, The Quaker Oats Company*
S. Rebecca Holland, *Treatment Alternatives for Safer Communities, Inc.*
Karin Kizer
Rebecca Morales, *University of Illinois at Chicago*
Prexy Nesbitt, *Francis Parker School*
Richard Newman, *Lake Forest Capital Management Company*
Allan Noonan, *U.S. Public Health Service*
Jewell Oates, *Women's Treatment Center*

Mary Page, *MacArthur Foundation*
Robert H. Puckett, *Indiana State University*
Martin Rabinowitch, *MacArthur Foundation*
Victor Rabinowitch, *MacArthur Foundation*
Raymond Risley, *Chicago Police Department*
Miguel Ruiz-Cabañas, *Mexican Foreign Ministry*
Mary Scott-Boria, *Youth Service Project, Inc.*
Adele Simmons, *MacArthur Foundation*
John Walsh-Alker, *Drug Strategies*
Woodward Wickham, *MacArthur Foundation*
Wayne Wiebel, *University of Illinois at Chicago*

MIAMI, FLORIDA
OCTOBER 29, 1996

Host: Edward T. Foote II,
               University of Miami

Comments: Mathea Falco, *Drug Strategies*

               Eduardo A. Gamarra,
               Florida International University

               Ambler Moss, *University of Miami*

Participants concurred that U.S. international drug
control policy should be built on a strong, comprehensive domestic strategy that effectively reduces
American demand for drugs. In that sense, the group
noted, foreign policy cannot be separated from domestic efforts. The United States is now both a consumer
and producer of illicit drugs: high potency "boutique"

marijuana grown in Humboldt County, California is sold to wealthy youth in Mexico City. From the Miami perspective, drug traffickers again threaten the security of the Caribbean, but now involve more sophisticated transnational narco-criminal networks than in earlier decades. Specifically, drugs move from Colombia through the Caribbean, Puerto Rico, Cuba and the Dominican Republic, which has become a key distribution point for cocaine in the eastern United States. Italian crime organizations are trafficking Bolivian cocaine out of Argentina, while Russian banks are laundering money in Aruba. Participants observed that small nations can literally be purchased, particularly when solid economic alternatives are not available. Poverty in Latin America and the Caribbean has increased substantially in recent years, making these countries more vulnerable to drug production and trafficking. One member reminded the group that Asia also has rapidly escalating drug problems. In China, where heroin addiction has increased 80 percent, the head of public security in Yunnan Province is seeking to develop effective treatment programs because he recognizes that reducing the demand for drugs is the key to success.

Money laundering, which has become a major problem in many countries, is particularly apparent in Miami. One expert noted that approximately one-fifth of Latin American drug profits go back to the producing countries while the rest remains in U.S. banks: for example, cash purchases of cars in Miami exceeded $200 million last year, although a city of this size would normally produce cash car sales of only $2 million. (These cars are then smuggled into Latin America for resale.)

The annual certification of other countries for their narcotics control cooperation has not been helpful, according to several members, because the process reinforces the image of the United States as "policeman of the world" without producing measurable results. The group concurred that U.S. drug policy has relied too much on bilateral approaches that attempt to pressure other governments to take action that might not be in their own interests: one participant noted that the United States treats its Latin neighbors as second class countries. The group concluded that the United States should engage other governments as partners, through multilateral and regional coalitions, and work together to reduce drug addiction and the power of the drug traffickers. One example of this kind of approach is the new Panama coalition, led by Panama's First Lady, modeled after the Miami Coalition which brings together business, political and civic leaders to develop community anti-drug strategies.

MIAMI MEETING PARTICIPANTS

Mae Bryant, *Metro-Dade Department of Human Services*

Marilyn Wagner Culp, *The Miami Coalition For A Safe and Drug-Free Community*

Christopher Deverell, *BM&A Ltd.*

Dennis Fagan, *U.S. Customs Office, Miami*

Mathea Falco, *Drug Strategies*

Edward T. Foote II, *University of Miami*

Eduardo Gamarra, *Florida International University*

Pedro José Greer, *University of Miami*

James Hall, *Up Front Information Services, Inc.*

Major Doug Hughes, *High Intensity Drug Trafficking Area Task Force*

Judge Herbert Klein, *Wetherington, Klein & Hubbart*
Clyde B. McCoy, *Comprehensive Drug*
 Research Center
Ambler Moss, *University of Miami*
Charles B. Reed, *State University System of Florida*
Don Shoemaker, *Council on Foreign Relations*
Susie Shoemaker, *Council on Foreign Relations*
David S. Weinstein, *Florida State Attorney's Office*
Charles Zwick, *retired Chairman,*
 Southeast Banking Corporation

ATLANTA, GEORGIA
NOVEMBER 18, 1996

Host: Harry G. Barnes, Jr.,
               The Carter Center

Comments: Mathea Falco, *Drug Strategies*

               Robert Pastor, *The Carter Center*

The group concurred that U.S. anti-drug policy had not
been successful in reducing drug purity or in increasing drug prices—the key goals of international supply
reduction initiatives. Yet the strategy has remained
essentially the same, emphasizing interdiction and
source-country eradication and enforcement. Some
members noted that even greater resources and better
implementation would not effectively reduce foreign
supplies of drugs coming into the United States. Drugs
can be produced very cheaply almost anywhere in the

world. When one source is disrupted, another soon takes its place. For example, the Cali cocaine cartel quickly took over the business of the Medellín cartel after its leaders were arrested and imprisoned. Although cocaine prices rose somewhat after the arrests, they dropped again to their former levels within six months. Another member noted that illicit U.S. production of marijuana has more than compensated for marijuana seized in transit from Latin America.

Participants in the Atlanta meeting voiced concern about the economics of the illicit drug trade, which generates enormous untaxed profits that might otherwise be invested in legitimate jobs and industry. Drug money, which circulates through a vast electronic banking system that supports total daily transfers in excess of $1 trillion, is often hard to detect. The drug traffic depends on "an audience held captive by addiction," according to one member, who noted that "rich or poor, black or white, all consumers are in the most basic sense a source of money."

From the Atlanta perspective, the lack of investment in prevention is a major problem. Grassroots organizations lack the money, technology, and expertise to impact public policy. As a result, less than one-third of high school students have any drug prevention programs; minority students in inner-city schools do not have access to the most effective teaching. Several members observed that politicians find it expedient to blame inner cities and foreign countries for drug trafficking while also being critical of social and educational programs that will alleviate the inner city drug problem. Instead they build more prisons, where structural racism and inequality ensure that incarcerated populations are disproportionately racial minorities. "Race and class fragment the political climate and serve to counter the capacity of society to intervene," according to one civic leader. Yet, prevention can work, as demonstrated by the success of anti-smoking efforts, built on a close collaboration between government and civil society.

Stricter penalties for offenders and traffickers have not dissuaded use or deterred trafficking. The Singapore model, which imposes capital punishment for drug dealing, would not be acceptable in this country. The group agreed that drugs must be addressed as both a national and a community problem with adverse effects on society, including corruption, violence, and social disruption. The problem must also be "desegregated" along class and racial lines to concentrate instead on the corporate structure of the drug business.

The Atlanta group reached a general consensus that international strategies should be re-evaluated and that much higher priority should be accorded to domestic prevention and education efforts. In addition, the media should be used as an instrument for shaping social values in relation to drug use and drug dealing and for discouraging the demand for drugs.

ATLANTA MEETING PARTICIPANTS

Harry G. Barnes, Jr., *The Carter Center*
Al Bartell, *The Carter Center*
Kris Bosworth, *U.S. Centers for Disease Control and Prevention*
Russell Broda, *Robinson-Humphrey Company, Inc.*
Christopher Burdett, *The Carter Center*
David Carroll, *The Carter Center*

Herschelle Challenor, *Clark Atlanta University*
Archie Crain, *Boy Scouts of America*
Kenneth A. Cutshaw, *Smith, Gambrell & Russell*
Mathea Falco, *Drug Strategies*
Gordon Giffin, *Long, Aldridge & Norman*
Lynn Walker Huntley, *Southern Education
  Foundation*
Walter R. Huntley, Jr., *Atlanta Economic
  Development Corporation*
Sandra MacKey, *author*
Wilmer (Buddy) Parker, *Assistant U.S. Attorney*
Margaret M. Pastor, *consultant*
Robert Pastor, *The Carter Center*
Gordon L. Streeb, *The Carter Center*
Adam Taylor, *The Carter Center*
David Worley, *attorney*

RESOURCES

Elena H. Alvarez, "Economic Development, Restructuring and the Illicit Drug Sector in Bolivia and Peru: Current Policies," *Journal of Interamerican Studies and World Affairs*. Vol. 37, No. 3. Fall 1995, pp. 125- 146.

Andean Information Network, *Human Rights Violations Stemming from the "War on Drugs" in Bolivia*. La Paz, Bolivia: Andean Information Network, 1993.

Peter Andreas, Eva Bertram, Morris Blachman, and Kenneth Sharpe, "Dead End Drug Wars," *Foreign Policy*, No. 85. 1991-1992, pp. 106- 128.

——————, *Drug War Politics: The Price of Denial*. Berkeley, CA: University of California Press, 1996.

Patrick L. Clawson and Rensselaer Lee III, *The Andean Cocaine Industry*. New York: St. Martin's Press, 1996.

Mathea Falco, "Passing Grades," *Foreign Affairs*. Vol. 74, No. 5. September /October 1995, pp. 15-20.

——————, "U.S. Drug Policy: Addicted to Failure," *Foreign Policy*. No. 102. Spring 1996, pp. 120-133.

——————, *The Making of A Drug Free America: Programs That Work*. New York: Times Books, 1994.

Stephen Flynn, "Worldwide Drug Scourge," *The Brookings Review*. Vol. 11, No. 1. Winter 1993, pp. 6- 11.

William C. Gilmore, *Dirty Money: The Evolution of Money Laundering Counter-Measures*. Strasbourg: Council of Europe Press, 1995.

Foreign Service Journal, "America's Losing Drug Strategy." Vol. 73, No. 10. October 1996.

Eduardo A. Gamarra, *The System of Justice in Bolivia: An Institutional Analysis*. San José, Costa Rica: Center for the Administration of Justice, 1991.

Human Rights Watch/Americas, *State of War: Political Violence and Counterinsurgency in Colombia*. New York: Human Rights Watch, 1993.

——————, *Bolivia: Human Rights Violations and the War on Drugs.* Vol. 7, No. 8. New York: Human Rights Watch, 1995.

——————, *Bolivia Under Pressure: Human Rights Violations and Coca Eradication.* Vol. 8, No. 4. New York: Human Rights Watch, 1996.

Human Rights Watch/Americas and Human Rights Watch Arms Project, *Colombia's Killer Networks: The Military-Paramilitary Partnership and the United States.* New York, Human Rights Watch, 1997.

Inter-American Commission on Drug Policy, *Seizing Opportunities: Report of the Inter-American Commission on Drug Policy.* La Jolla, CA: Institute of the Americas and The Center for Iberian and Latin American Studies, June 1991.

International Narcotics Control Board, *Report of the International Narcotics Control Board for 1995.* Vienna: United Nations, 1996.

Jeffrey Laurenti, *Breaking the Drug Chain: Options for International Policy on Narcotic Drugs.* New York: United Nations Association of the USA, 1990.

Rensselaer W. Lee III, *The White Labyrinth: Cocaine and Political Power.* New Brunswick, NJ: Transaction Publishers, 1989.

Mark H. Moore, "Supply Reduction and Drug Law Enforcement," Michael Tonry and James Q. Wilson, eds., *Drugs and Crime.* Chicago: University of Chicago Press, 1990, pp. 109-157.

David F. Musto, *The American Disease: Origins of Narcotic Control.* New York: Oxford University Press, 1987.

Douglas W. Payne, "Drugs into Money into Power," *Freedom Review.* Vol. 27, No. 4. July-August 1996, pp. 9-104.

Peter Reuter, *The Limits and Consequences of U.S. Foreign Drug Control Efforts.* Santa Monica, CA: RAND, 1992.

Peter Reuter, Gordon Crawford, and Jonathan Cave, *Sealing the Borders: The Effects of Increased Military Participation in Drug Interdiction.* Santa Monica, CA: RAND, 1988.

K. Jack Riley, *Snow Job? The War Against International Cocaine Trafficking.* New Brunswick, NJ: Transaction Publishers, 1996.

C. Peter Rydell and Susan S. Everingham, *Controlling Cocaine: Supply Versus Demand Programs*. Santa Monica, CA: RAND, 1994.

Eric Schlosser, "Reefer Madness," *The Atlantic Monthly*. August 1994, pp. 45-63.

Peter H. Smith, ed., *Drug Policy in the Americas*. Boulder, CO: Westview Press, 1992.

Paul B. Stares, *Global Habit: The Drug Problem in a Borderless World*. Washington, D.C.: The Brookings Institution, 1996.

Francisco E. Thoumi, *Political Economy and Illegal Drugs in Colombia*. Boulder, CO: Lynne Rienner Publishers Inc., 1995

Washington Office on Latin America, *Clear and Present Dangers: The U.S. Military and the War on Drugs in the Andes*. Washington, D.C.: Washington Office on Latin America, 1991.

——————, *The Colombian National Police, Human Rights and U.S. Drug Policy*. Washington, D.C.: Washington Office on Latin America, 1993.

Phil Williams and Ernesto U. Savona, eds., *The United Nations and Transnational Organized Crime*. London: Frank Cass, 1996.

Coletta Youngers, *The Andean Quagmire: Rethinking U.S. Drug Control Efforts in the Andes*. Washington, D.C.: Washington Office on Latin America, 1996.

U.S. Government Publications

Bureau for International Narcotics and Law Enforcement Affairs (Department of State), *International Narcotics Control Strategy Report, 1996*. Washington, D.C.: Department of State, March 1996.

Bureau of Intelligence and Research (Department of State) and Central Intelligence Agency, *Conference Report: Economics of the Narcotics Industry*. Washington, D.C.: Department of State, 1994.

Department of Health and Human Services, *National Survey Results on Drug Abuse from the Monitoring the Future Study (1975-1995)*. Rockville, MD: National Institute on Drug Abuse, 1996.

General Accounting Office, *The Drug War: Colombia Is Undertaking Antidrug Programs, but Impact Is Uncertain*. GAO/NSIAD-93-158. Washington, D.C.: GAO, August 1993.

——————, *Drug Control: Interdiction Efforts in Central America Have Had Little Impact on the Flow of Drugs*. GAO/NSIAD-94-233. Washington, D.C.: GAO, August 1994.

——————, *Drug War: Observations on U.S. International Drug Control Efforts*. Congressional testimony of Joseph E. Kelly, GAO Director of International Affairs Issues. GAO/T-NSIAD-95-194. Washington, D.C.: GAO, August 1995.

——————, *Drug Control: Counternarcotics Efforts in Mexico*. GAO/NSIAD-96-163. Washington, D.C.: GAO, June 1996.

Office of National Drug Control Policy, *Crop Substitution in the Andes*. Washington, D.C.: ONDCP, December 1993.

——————, *What America's Users Spend on Illegal Drugs, 1988-1993*. Washington, D.C.: U.S. Government Printing Office, Spring 1995.

——————, *The National Drug Control Strategy: 1996*. Washington, D.C.: U.S. Government Printing Office, 1996.

Office of Technology Assessment, *Alternative Coca Reduction Strategies in the Andean Region*. Washington, D.C.: U.S. Government Printing Office, July 1993.

79